SCIENCE FILES

METALS

SCIENCE FILES – METALS
was produced by

David West 👫 **Children's Books**
7 Princeton Court
55 Felsham Road
London SW15 1AZ

Designers: Rob Shone, Fiona Thorne, David West
Editor: James Pickering
Picture Research: Carrie Haines

First published in Great Britain in 2001 by
Heinemann Library, Halley Court, Jordan Hill,
Oxford OX2 8EJ, a division of Reed Educational and
Professional Publishing Limited.

OXFORD MELBOURNE AUCKLAND
JOHANNESBURG BLANTYRE GABORONE
IBADAN PORTSMOUTH (NH) USA CHICAGO

05 04 03 02 01
10 9 8 7 6 5 4 3 2 1

ISBN 0 431 14302 1 (HB)
ISBN 0 431 14308 0 (PB)

British Library Cataloguing in Publication Data

Parker, Steve, 1952 -
  Metal. - (Science files)
  1. Metals
  I. Title
  620.1'6

Printed and bound in Spain by Bookprint, S.L., Barcelona

PHOTO CREDITS :
Abbreviations: t-top, m-middle, b-bottom, r-right,
l-left.

Front cover - tr (Dr Morley Read) - Science Photo
Library. 4tr & 8tr (A.C. Waltham), 10bl (Peter
Scholey), 18bl (Earl Young), 19ml (Maximilian Stock
Ltd), 20bl (Jeff Greenberg@uno.com), 22tr (S.
Bavister), 23bl & t, 24br & 26r (Bildagentur
Schuster/Schiller), 5tr (Robert Frerck), 9tl, 17tl,
18/19t, 19m, 21br - Robert Harding Picture Library.
8bl (US Dept of Energy), 4/5b & 10tr (Rosenfeld
Images Ltd), 14tr (Astrid and Hanns-Frieder Michler),
24tr (Dr Morley Read), 25br (Peter Thorne/Johnson
Matthey), 27tr (Vaughan Fleming), 6/7b, 28br -
Science Photo Library. 7br & 11br (Eileen
Tweedy/London Museum), 19br (Deir-ez-Zor
Museum, Syria/Dagli Orti), 24bl (British Library) -
The Art Archive. 14m & 27mr (H. Halberstadt) - The
Stock Market. 15br - AKG London. 26b Hulton-
Archive. 27bl - Allsport.

Every effort has been made to trace the copyright
holders and we apologise in advance for any
unintentional omissions. We would be pleased to
insert the appropriate acknowledgement in any
subsequent edition of this publication.

*An explanation of difficult words can be
found in the glossary on page 30.*

SCIENCE FILES

METALS

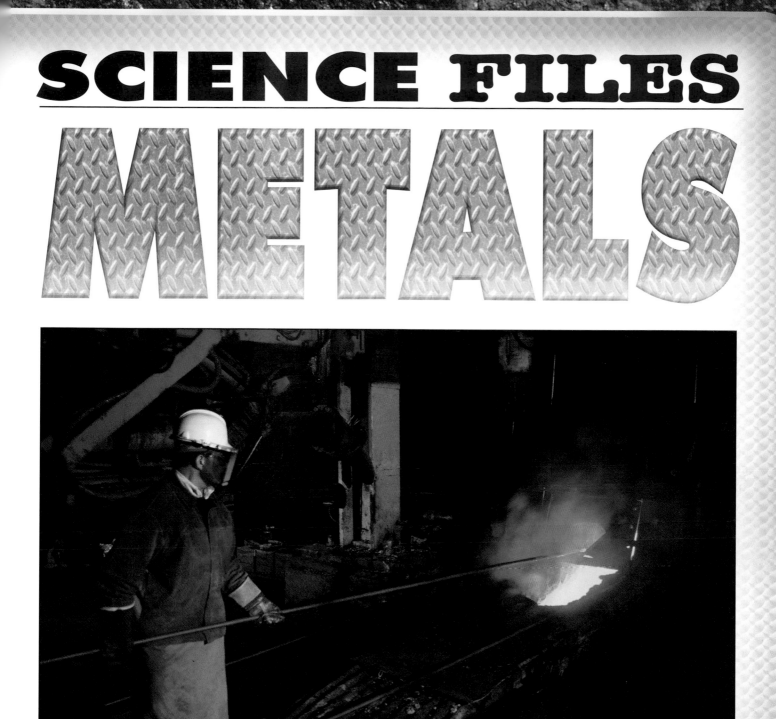

Steve Parker

Heinemann
LIBRARY

CONTENTS

Most metals come from the Earth's rocks. The rocks which are rich in metals are known as ores. They are dug up or mined. These rocks are being mined because they contain the metal copper.

To obtain a metal from its ore rock, the rock is usually mixed with various chemicals and heated in a furnace. The ore melts and the pure metal flows out.

INTRODUCTION

Why is a golden crown similar to a car, a jumbo jet, a drawing pin, and the girders of a skyscraper? They are all made of metals. Most metals are hard, strong, shiny and long-lasting. Dozens of different metals are vital in our modern world. Some are used in huge amounts, like iron and aluminium. Others are used in tiny quantities, like tungsten and palladium. We obtain metals from the Earth's rocks. Getting metals out of the rocks uses huge amounts of energy, and the supply of metal-containing rocks is limited. So it's vital to conserve and recycle metals for the future.

Some rare metals are valued for their beauty. This small statue from Peru is made of gold.

Some metals are common and valued for practical uses. These car bodies are made from steel, which is mostly the metal iron added to other substances, chiefly carbon.

Very rarely, a metal such as gold, silver or copper is found as an almost pure lump, called a nugget, lying on the ground. But most metals are joined or combined with various other substances, and spread thinly through the rocks of the Earth.

METAL ORES

A rock which is rich in a certain metal, and so worth digging up to obtain the metal, is known as an ore. Scientists called geologists test rocks to see which metals they contain, and whether they should be mined.

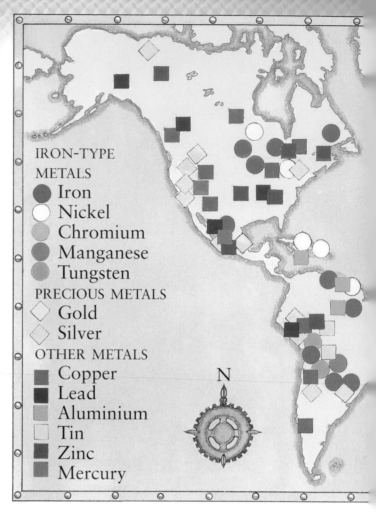

IRON-TYPE METALS
- ● Iron
- ○ Nickel
- ● Chromium
- ● Manganese
- ● Tungsten

PRECIOUS METALS
- ◇ Gold
- ◇ Silver

OTHER METALS
- ■ Copper
- ■ Lead
- ■ Aluminium
- □ Tin
- ■ Zinc
- ■ Mercury

N

The coloured shapes on this map show which metals are found in ores around the world. In fact, most metals occur in most places. But not all ores are rich enough in metals to make them worth mining. Many remote parts of the world are still being explored for metal ores and other minerals.

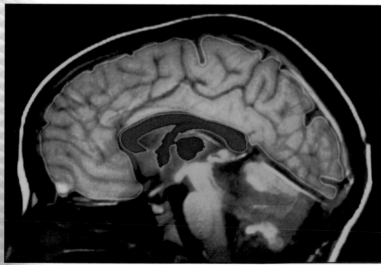

Sodium and potassium are needed for the nerves and brain to work, and calcium for healthy bones. This image is a scan of the brain.

WHERE METAL ORES ARE FOUND

In the Earth's rocky outer layer, or crust, about 25% (one-quarter) of the substances are metals. Aluminium is most common, then iron.

Other metals 0.13%

Aluminium 8.07%

Iron 5.06%

Titanium 0.62%

Magnesium 2.07%

Calcium 3.64%

Sodium 2.83%

75% of crust is non-metal

Potassium 2.58%

LOOKING FOR METAL ORES

Geologists use many methods to search, or prospect, for rocks rich in metals. Photographs taken by satellites in space show how some rocks form in certain shapes or layers, which suggest they contain metals. Also, large clumps of ores affect the Earth's gravity (pulling effect) or natural magnetism. Very sensitive detectors measure how these forces vary.

Many tests are needed to check rocks for metals. This rock seems to contain gold. But it is another, worthless substance, 'fool's gold'.

Facts from the PAST

Certain metals were so important to people in ancient times, that periods of history are named after them. After the Stone Age, the first main 'metal age' was the Bronze Age. It began over 5,000 years ago in Western Asia (the Near East).

A bronze spear tip from Europe.

8 MINING METALS

The rocks called ores, which are rich in metals, are mined from the ground in many ways. Soft ores at the Earth's surface can be scooped up. Other ores are dug from tunnels hundreds of metres below the surface, using powerful drills, cutters, and explosives such as dynamite.

ORES AT THE SURFACE

Digging ores at the surface is called open-cast mining. This is done for several metals, including copper, aluminium and iron. The ore is loosened and broken up by dynamite blasts or drills. It is loaded on to huge trucks by giant excavators which can lift tens of tonnes in one bucket-load.

Geologists bore holes using tube-shaped drills, to obtain 'rods' of rock called cores. Each core of ore is tested for the metals it contains, and how much of them.

The Bingham Canyon open cast mine for copper ore, in the USA, is the world's largest man-made hole. It is more than 600 metres deep.

HOW ORES FORM

Why do some rocks contain more metals than others? Deep underground is magma – rock so hot that it's melted and runny (1). Rocks form from cooling magma, leaving a mixture of hot water and metal particles. This runs into nearby rocks (2) and the metals are deposited. Rain water seeps into the ground carrying the metals to spongy parts of rock (3). Metals may collect in the volcano's lava (4). Rivers wash metals and other minerals out of rocks, to settle in lakes and seas (5). Or water far below the ocean floor carries metals upwards into cracks (6) or into springs in the sea bed (7).

Mining for iron ore in Sweden's Kiruna region takes place deep underground in very hot and humid conditions.

ORES DEEP UNDERGROUND

Many ores are found as narrow layers of rock, called veins or seams. Often, these are not level, but tilted. Mining the ore is easier at the surface. As the layer dips deeper, vertical shafts and horizontal tunnels must be dug to reach it. The ore is broken up by drills or saw-bladed cutters. Or holes are drilled in the rock for sticks of explosives, then everyone moves along tunnels to a safe distance, and BANG!

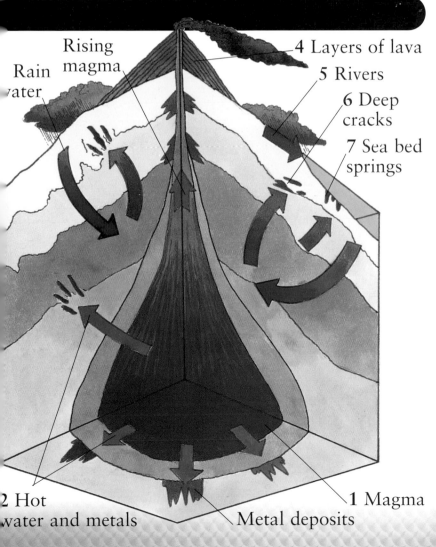

Rising magma

Rain water

4 Layers of lava

5 Rivers

6 Deep cracks

7 Sea bed springs

2 Hot water and metals

1 Magma

Metal deposits

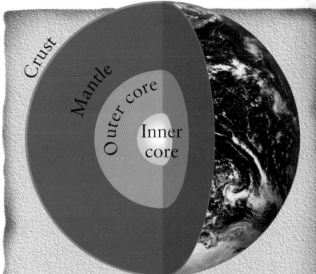

Crust

Mantle

Outer core

Inner core

Ideas for the **FUTURE**

The Earth's centre, or core, consists mainly of two metals – most is iron, with some nickel. Their quantities are so vast, they would supply our industries almost for ever. But reaching them means drilling through the Earth's middle layer, the mantle. At 2,900 kilometres thick, that would take almost for ever, too!

9

The most widely used metal in the world is iron. However, very little of it is used in the form of pure iron. Most is added to other substances, especially carbon, to make steel.

A HUGE INDUSTRY

Iron is so important that mining its ores, and refining them, to get out or extract the metal, is one of the world's biggest industries. In rocks, iron is usually in other forms because it is combined with other substances, such as oxygen (as iron oxides) and sulphur (as iron sulphides).

THE BLAST FURNACE

Iron ore arrives by road, rail or ship. It is ground up and mixed with coke (which is made by controlled burning of coal) and limestone. The three raw materials tip into the top of the blast furnace, a huge tower over 30 metres tall. The coke burns in blasts of hot air at well above 1,000°C, to melt the ore.

Impurities collect as slag. The mostly pure metal, called pig iron, is taken away to make steel (see next page).

Iron was a vital part of the Industrial Revolution, in the late 1700s. The first iron bridge was built in Shropshire, UK.

1 Iron ore

2 Coke

3 Limestone

4 Raw materials blended into charge

As the iron ore melts, the iron forms a separate layer. Workers take regular samples to test the melt for purity. They must wear special clothes against the intense heat, up to 1,500°C.

SMELTING

Like most metals, iron is extracted by the basic process of smelting, or heating, its ores. This happens in a giant oven called the blast furnace. The fuel burned to make the heat is coke. This also provides substances to combine with the oxygen, sulphur and other chemicals which were joined to the iron. This allows the iron to become free. Limestone soaks up or absorbs these various substances to leave fairly pure iron.

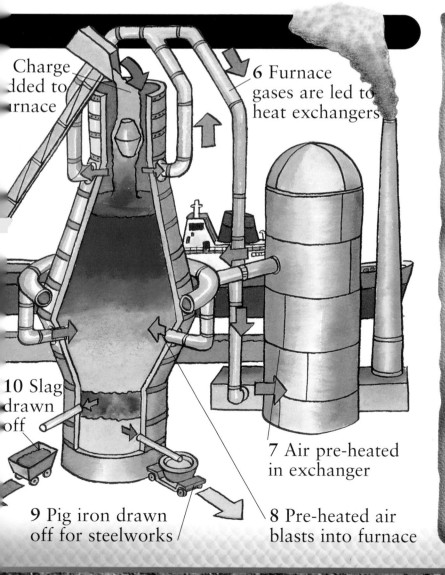

Charge added to furnace

6 Furnace gases are led to heat exchangers

10 Slag drawn off

7 Air pre-heated in exchanger

9 Pig iron drawn off for steelworks

8 Pre-heated air blasts into furnace

Facts from the PAST

The Iron Age began at different times in different regions. The Hittite people of Anatolia (now Turkey) were the first to smelt ores and make fairly pure, tough iron, some 3,200 years ago. Methods spread through Europe from 2,800 years ago. The technique of shaping iron by forging became common about 2,500 years ago.

Iron axe and spear heads from the Iron Age.

Aluminium is very light, fairly soft and easily ben Millions of drinks cans are made from it daily.

Most metals are obtained or extracted from their ores by heating, or smelting (see page 11). However, this does not always produce very pure metal. So further methods are used, which are called refining the metal.

Copper carries, or conducts, electricity very well. So it is used to make electrical cables and wires.

COPPER

Copper is obtained in two stages. First its ores are crushed, mixed with water and frothing chemicals, filtered, and smelted at 1,500°C with blasts of air and chemicals called fluxes. The result is copper which is 98–99% pure. The next stage is refining by electrolysis (see 'Aluminium from its ore'). This increases the purity to almost 100%.

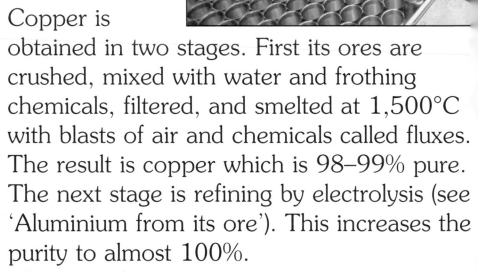

Testing nickel, which will be made into coins.

NICKEL

The very hard, shiny metal called nickel does not melt until the temperature is 1,455°C. So nickel ores must be heated much hotter than most other metal ores.

Aluminium is the second most widely used metal, after iron. Its main ore is bauxite, which is treated, mixed and heated with chemicals to part-process it, into sugar-like crystals called alumina (aluminium oxide). These are added to a substance called cryolite, which is heated to 980°C in troughs known as reduction pots. Huge amounts of electricity, about enough to power a whole city, are passed through the mix. This makes the aluminium separate from the oxygen, in a process called electrolysis.

In the reduction pots, alumina is separated into oxygen and pure, molten aluminium.

3 Bauxite and caustic soda heated in precipitator

2 Ground-up bauxite

6 Alumina crystals dried in kilns at 1,000°C

5 Impurities removed in settling tank

4 Mixture is filtered

7 Cryolite added

8 Alumina is purified by electrolysis with cryolite in reduction pots

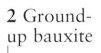

1 Caustic soda and other chemicals

9 Ingots (bars) of pure aluminium

In this close-up of a nickel-silver alloy, micro-blobs of silver are held in a sheet or matrix of nickel.

Many metals are extracted and refined from their ores, to make them pure, and then added to other substances again. This is because mixing metals with certain substances can give them extra features, such as greater strength.

MANY MIXES

A metal which is carefully mixed or blended with another substance is called an alloy. The other substance may be a non-metal, like carbon, or another metal.

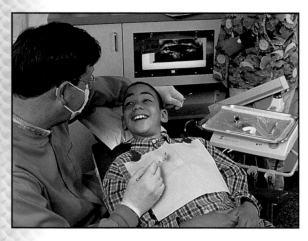

A 'gold' dental filling may be an alloy of the metals chromium, cobalt, titanium and molybdenum.

ALLOYS OF COPPER

Copper is used to make many alloys, with features such as ease of shaping and resistance to corrosion. The amounts of metal are carefully controlled. Brass that contains about one-fifth zinc is yellow-orange and can be shaped when cold. Brass with almost one-half zinc is whitish and shaped when hot. Small amounts of other metals may be added too, such as lead to bronze.

COPPER	COPPER	COPPER	COPPER
TIN	TIN	ZINC	NICKEL
ZINC			

GUNMETAL   BRONZE   BRASS   CUPRONICKEL

NEW ALLOYS

Some types of new alloys are called superplastic alloys. They can stretch to twice their length, like elastic, yet stay very hard and strong. Other types of alloy are known as superconductors. They carry electricity almost perfectly.

'Silver' and 'copper' coins are not pure metals, but alloys such as silvery, hard-wearing cupronickel.

Earphones contain tiny but powerful magnets of cobalt-samarium alloy. Without this alloy, the earphones would be huge!

Facts from the PAST

Some alloys of copper, such as bronze, were known in ancient times. Perhaps this is because copper often occurs in ores with other metals, so alloys form naturally as the ore is smelted. One poisonous metal-like substance in copper ore is arsenic. In the past, many people must have died from it while purifying copper, without realizing the cause.

A bronze helmet from Roman times.

Alloys are metals blended or mixed with other substances. The most-used metal, iron, is mixed with another substance, carbon. The result is the world's most widespread alloy – steel.

LOTS OF STEELS

There are thousands of kinds of steel. Each is based on iron, plus varying amounts of carbon, plus other metals and substances. Standard carbon or plate steel is iron with up to 1/50 carbon. It is used for mass production of items such as vehicle bodies and the cases of washing machines. Many 'tin' cans are made from plate steel coated with a thin layer of tin to stop the steel rusting or corroding.

The girders and beams for the frame of a skyscraper are made from steel which is very strong and stiff, and able to bear great weight. This is high-tensile steel.

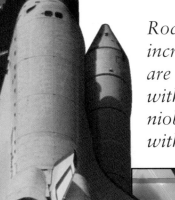

Rocket and jet engines produce incredible heat. Their casings are made from special steels, with added metals such as niobium and titanium, to withstand the temperature.

Ideas for the FUTUR

Steel is strong, but not transparent (see-through). Glass is the opposite, weak but transparent. One day, a new steel alloy will be both strong and see-through. It could cover whole cities to keep out the bad weather.

There are many ways to change pig iron (see pages 10–11) into steel. In the basic oxygen process, oxygen is blasted at high pressure for about 20 minutes, over a pool of melted pig and scrap iron, in the bottom of a giant, flask-shaped, tilting furnace. The oxygen alters the amount of carbon in the iron. The resulting steel is poured out as a huge blob weighing 300 tonnes or more, at a temperature of 1,625°C.

2 Oxygen pumped in

Lime

3 Oxygen blows from end of lance over molten iron

4 Furnace tilts to pour steel into ladle

1 Bath of molten pig iron and scrap iron

5 Molten steel is taken for stirring and refining

Molten steel pours into a huge ladle.

City dome of 'Stlass' (transparent steel).

STAINLESS STEELS

One important group of steel alloys is stainless steels. These have added amounts of the shiny metal chromium to make them very hard and smooth. They resist scratches, stains and corrosion. They are used for cutlery, sinks and industrial containers.

Metals seem so hard and strong, that they are impossible to bend, squeeze and alter into certain shapes. But there are many ways of shaping metals – usually with very powerful industrial machinery made of even stronger metals.

A molten rod of titanium is drawn or pulled through narrowing holes until it is the required thickness. Titanium is one of the hardest and strongest metals.

CHOOSING THE METAL

Each kind of metal has its own special features, which make it suitable for shaping in a certain way. For example, copper is very ductile. This means it can be pulled or drawn into long, thin shapes like wires and tubes. Gold and silver are also ductile, and they are malleable, too. This means they can be pressed or hammered into very thin sheets, even when cold.

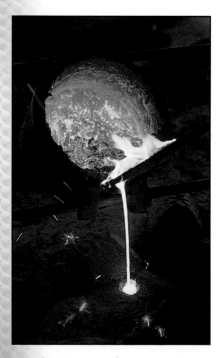

Molten metal is cast in a hollow mould of sand, to cool and harden. The sand will be crumbled and re-used.

SHAPING HOT METALS

As a metal is heated, it becomes softer. So most metals are shaped hot, as they come out of the furnace where they are made. They can be squeezed into thin sheets by massive rollers, hammered at the forge, squirted or pulled (drawn) through narrow holes, or cast by pouring into a hollow shape to cool and become solid.

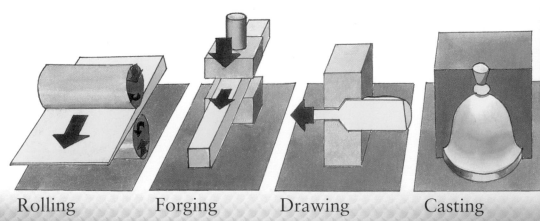

Rolling   Forging   Drawing   Casting

TEMPERING AND TIPPING

Even after a metal object is shaped, it can be altered in various ways. In tempering, the object is heated to a certain temperature, then suddenly 'quenched' or cooled, by plunging it into water or oil. Tempering is used especially for steel alloys and makes them harder and stronger. For greater toughness, another metal may be added. Saw blades and drill bits are usually steel, but their tips and edges may be made of the even harder-wearing metal, tungsten.

Measuring parts for engines, which must be machined to a thousandth of a millimetre.

Items such as can lids and bottle tops are stamped from sheets. The leftover parts of the sheets are melted and recycled.

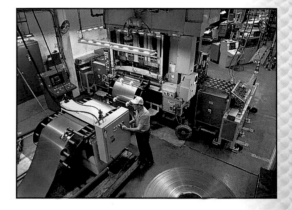

SHAPING COLD METALS

Softer metals, such as aluminium, tin and mild steel, are shaped while cold. Machining removes metal using drills, grinders and burrs. A lump of metal can be forced, or extruded, through a hole or inside a mould, to form a long shape. Presses bend and squeeze with great power. Stamps chop or press out shapes from a sheet.

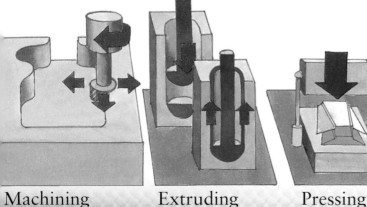

Machining   Extruding   Pressing   Stamping

Facts from the
PAST

Copper was mined and hammered into shape more than 7,000 years ago. However, it was too soft to make strong, sharp blades and edges. It gave way to its alloy, bronze.

Copper statuette, 7th century BC.

19

We cut some materials, such as paper, with scissors or other blades. We also join them in various ways, such as using tape or glue. We cut and join metals in many ways, too. But the tools we use are much stronger and more powerful.

CUTTING

Metals like steel are hard. But there's usually another substance which is even harder, such as the metal tungsten, or the substances silicon carbide or diamond. So these can cut through most metals by sawing or grinding. Great heat from a furnace, blow-torch or laser beam softens metals, so they can be cut more easily, or the heat even burns right through them.

When cutting or welding metal, there is great heat, and sparks fly. It's vital to wear protective equipment.

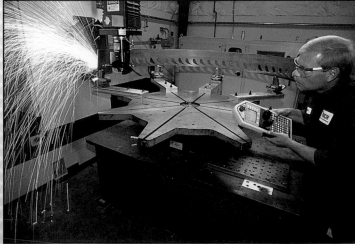

Very powerful laser beams, using the gas carbon dioxide, can heat metals to thousands of degrees. The beam is narrow and melts only a small patch of metal, so the cut is very accurate.

JOINED BY HEAT AND PRESSURE

A substance squashed under pressure gets very hot. Friction welding rubs together two metal items, which become so heated that they join together. Very hot burning gases (metal inert gas, MIG) or an electrical spark, or arc, also weld metal parts together.

Friction weld   MIG weld   Arc weld

Rivets are like very short nails, with their ends hammered over, almost flat.

JOINING

If a metal is heated enough, it starts to melt and go runny. When two almost-melted metal edges flow together, and then go cool, the result is a very strong joint, called a weld. Metal parts can also be joined by glue, solder, bolts or rivets.

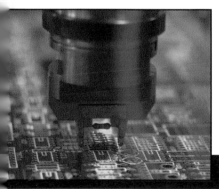

Solder is a soft alloy that melts at a fairly low temperature, about 200°C. It is used like 'glue' to join delicate electrical parts.

The heat from a powerful laser beam not only cuts through metal. It also melts the edges of metal parts to a jelly. The edges flow together and cool to form the joint. Sudden and extremely high pressure from an explosive, or from hammer blows when forging heated metal, has the same melting effect.

Ideas for the FUTURE

Different glues can join most substances strongly. But even superglues cannot fix certain metals. Perhaps a new glue will be able to melt the edges of metal parts, so they weld. Then we can stick together car parts at home!

Could future kit cars be glued?

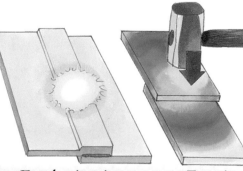

Laser beam   Explosive impact   Forging

21

Many metals are used in large amounts in factories. The main one is iron, used chiefly in the form of its alloy, steel. Other common industrial metals are aluminium, tin, copper, zinc, lead and chromium.

LIGHT BUT STRONG

Aluminium is very light, but fairly strong. Unlike iron and steel, it does not go rusty. It is widely used for all kinds of factory-made objects, from cooking pots and pans to ladders, high-power electrical cables and jumbo jets.

Chemicals containing certain metals burn fast and bright with coloured sparks. They are used in fireworks. Sodium is yellow, strontium is red, barium is green. Copper and cobalt are blue.

Most vehicle bodies are made from steel parts. These are relatively inexpensive, light and strong, and fairly easy to cut out, press into large curved shapes, and weld together. However, they must be protected or they will soon rust away.

Iron is not only made into huge objects. A thin coating of tiny iron-based particles is used on video and cassette tapes, to store information as micro-patches of magnetism.

ANTI-CORROSION

Iron and steel tend to corrode – go soft, weak and 'rotten', mainly with rust. Metals such as zinc, tin and chromium resist corrosion. So steel objects are often covered with a very thin layer of another metal, to protect against corrosion. One method is to melt the anti-corrosion metal in a bath, and dip the object into it. Another method is electroplating (see below). Items treated in this way with hard, shiny chromium are called 'chrome-plated'.

Facts from the PAST

Lead is very heavy, soft, easy to melt and bend, and resists corrosion. It was used for roofing and water pipes, in paints, for bullets, and as an extra substance or additive in petrol, to make engines run smoothly. But doctors discovered that lead is poisonous, causing brain damage. Now it is used much more rarely and with great care.

Lead shot (shotgun pellets).

ELECTROPLATING

Anti-corrosion zinc plating.

In electroplating, electricity is passed through liquid between two terminals, positive and negative. The positive terminal is made of the metal to make the covering layer, or plating. Tiny particles of the metal, called ions, detach from the terminal into the liquid. They are carried by the electricity to the negative terminal. This is made of the item which is to receive the coating or plating. The particles of metal stick firmly to it, forming an all-over layer of even thickness.

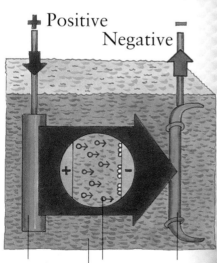

+ Positive

– Negative

Metal to do the plating | Ions | Object to be plated
Liquid

Silver and gold are very good conductors (carriers) of electricity, and also hard-wearing. They are used for high-quality electrical wires, switches and contacts.

Gold! Silver! Some metals have been desired through the ages. People search for years, travel vast distances, endure great hardship, even kill for them. Why?

WHY METALS ARE PRECIOUS

Gold, silver, platinum and similar metals are precious for several reasons. They have beautiful, glowing colours. They are shiny and long-lasting. They can be hammered and 'worked' in many ways, into tiny, delicate shapes such as rings, necklaces and bracelets. And they are rare in the rocks, taking much effort to find and purify. Owning these metals is a symbol of wealth and power.

Facts from the **PAST**

The alchemists of olden times believed there was a magic substance which would turn ordinary, cheap metals into pure gold. It was called the 'philosopher's stone'. Despite searching for 500 years, no one has ever discovered it.

Alchemists search for gold.

Chemicals containing silver are used in photographic and movie film. They change colour when light shines on them, to produce a picture or image on the film.

Tiny flakes and nuggets (lumps) of pure gold are sometimes found naturally, especially in river mud.

Gold is obtained from ores mined specially for the purpose, and also from slag – material left over after refining ores of other metals. The slag is washed by a high-pressure hose into a soup-like slurry. Particles containing gold are heavy and settle to the bottom. They are mixed with the chemical sodium cyanide, which takes up the gold and leaves behind other substances. Then the metal zinc is added, to join with the cyanide, leaving gold as free particles. These are pressed, dried and heated, to remove water and other impurities, then smelted in a furnace to yield gold.

2 Gold-containing particles settle in tanks

3 Particles are shaken with sodium cyanide

4 Mixture is filtered

5 Zinc is added to mixture

6 Cyanide is removed

1 Slag heap containing tiny particles of gold is washed with high-pressure hose, forming slurry.

7 Mixture is pressed, dried and roasted

8 Gold dust is smelted

METAL MONEY

Gold and silver were once used for coins, due to their great value and resistance to corrosion. Today their place has been taken by harder-wearing, less expensive alloys. But gold and silver bars, or ingots, are still used by banks in special cases.

Gold ingots.

There are more than 90 pure natural substances, called chemical elements. About 70 of these are metals. Many new discoveries in science and technology rely on rare metals, unfamiliar in daily life.

METAL CATS

Each new car has a 'cat'. This is a catalytic convertor, a device in the exhaust system. It makes the engine fumes cleaner, by changing polluting gases to cleaner substances. Car 'cats' work using rare metals such as palladium, platinum and rhodium.

Facts from the **PAST**

Polish-born French scientist Marie Curie did many experiments with metals. She was first to purify two, polonium and radium. She also discovered some metals naturally give off rays and particles, which we now know can cause great harm. She invented a new term for this feature: radioactivity.

Marie Curie (1867–1934).

Nuclear power stations use metals such as uranium or plutonium as fuel. Nuclear weapons use the same metals in a similar way.

BATTERY METALS

The diagram below shows some of the metals in a typical long-life battery, which is called an alkaline electrical cell. The rechargeable batteries known as nicads are named after the two main metals they contain, nickel and cadmium.

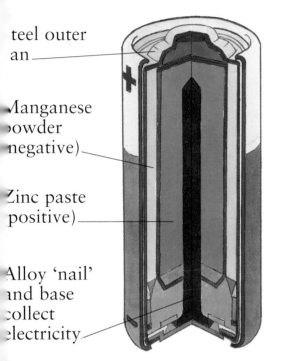

Steel outer can

Manganese powder (negative)

Zinc paste (positive)

Alloy 'nail' and base collect electricity

Mercury is one of the strangest metals. It melts from a solid at minus 39°C. At ordinary room temperature, it is a liquid. It is used in medical thermometers.

ELECTRICITY FROM METALS

Metals such as lead, zinc, manganese, lithium, mercury, nickel and cadmium are used in electrical batteries. They take part in the chemical processes which produce electricity. However, many of these metals are harmful if they 'escape' into soil or water. So old batteries must be disposed of properly, with great care. Rechargeable batteries, which can be used many times, help to reduce the waste and pollution caused by throwing away old batteries.

Billions are spent each year on alloy research. Rare metals are combined to make new alloys which are stronger, lighter and more resistant to wear, heat, rays and chemicals. They are used in hi-tech machinery such as racing cars, computers and aeroplanes.

In ancient times, people used only a few metals and their alloys, such as iron, copper, lead, tin, bronze and brass. Today we use nearly all of the metals that occur in nature – and some that do not.

The metal barium shows up white on an X-ray image. People swallow a 'soup' of it for a medical check-up.

ARTIFICIAL METALS

Some metals do not occur in nature. They are artificial or man-made, in massive 'atom-smasher' machines. These metals may have very specialized features such as amazing magnetism or great radioactivity. They could be used for future research in medicine, space, computers and other high-tech sciences.

Ideas for the FUTURE

Supplies of metals may be limited here on Earth. But deep in space, lumps of rock called asteroids are rich in various metals, such as iron, nickel and iridium. Now and then a lump of such rock falls to Earth as a meteorite. In future, we may send spacecraft to mine and refine these rocks, and bring back fresh supplies of metals.

Scientists need fast computers to aid their research. Superconductor alloys will speed up their equipment.

Meteorite which fell in Texas, USA

Many kinds of metals can be collected for recycling. This saves natural habitats, raw materials, energy, time, waste, pollution. These metals include iron and steel, aluminium, copper, lead, gold, silver and brass. Many new products, from cans to cars, have recyclable parts built into their designs.

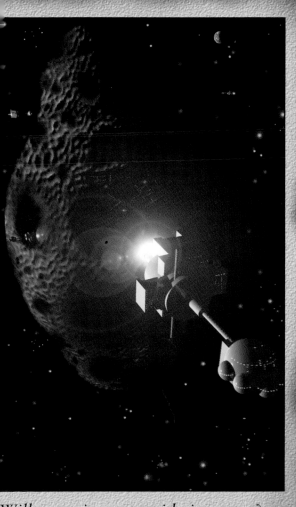

Will we mine asteroids in space?

METAL PROBLEMS

Extracting and refining metals from their ores uses up vast amounts of chemicals and raw materials, and also heat and other forms of energy. This energy comes mostly from coal, oil and gas – fuels which will soon be in short supply, if we continue to use them so fast. Also, open-cast ore mines scar the land, and giant piles of leftover rocks cause huge problems of waste and pollution.

SAVING METALS

In addition, we have already used much of the ore which is richest in metals. In the future, we will have to process more ore, to obtain less metal. These are just some of the reasons why saving and recycling metals are so important.

TYPE OF METAL		FEATURES AND USES
INDUSTRIAL METALS	Iron (*chemical symbol – Fe*)	Heavy, quite strong, magnetic, can be cast and forged, but rusts in damp conditions; used for decorative metalwork; most iron is combined with other metals and carbon to make steels
	Steel (alloys of iron)	Very strong; many different kinds used for girders, beams, frames, sheets, cars, appliances, machines, 'tin' cans, nuts, bolts, tools, cutlery, stainless ware, thousands of other items
	Aluminium (*Al*)	Light, strong, slightly brittle; used mainly as alloys in planes, electrical cables, lightweight parts, cans, cartons, cookware, foil
	Copper (*Cu*)	Conducts electricity well, resists corrosion; used for wires, tubes, cables, pipes, chemical containers, machine parts
	Tin (*Sn*)	Resists corrosion well; used to cover other metallic items such as steel containers ('tin' cans), by electroplating or dipping
PRECIOUS METALS	Gold (*Au*)	Very valuable, easily worked, resists corrosion; used for rings, bracelets and other kinds of jewellery, electroplating, coins, electrical equipment, heat shields, bearings, medicine
	Silver (*Ag*)	Valuable, easily worked, resists corrosion; used for electroplating, rings and jewellery, coins, electrical equipment
	Platinum (*Pt*)	Very tough and hard-wearing; used for bearings, machine parts, jewellery and scientific equipment
OTHER METALS	Mercury (*Hg*)	A silvery liquid at normal temperature; used in batteries and electrical equipment, chemicals, thermometers, dentistry
	Cadmium (*Cd*)	Fairly soft and silvery, similar to zinc; used for electroplating, alloys that melt at low temperatures (as in fire alarms)
	Nickel (*Ni*)	Hard, silvery-white; used in alloys, as electroplating to prevent wear and corrosion, for chemical reactions, in super-magnets
	Chromium (*Cr*)	Extremely hard, tough and shiny; used to electroplate and protect other items, in bearings, moving parts and stainless steel
	Ytterbium (*Yb*)	A rare, silvery metal with almost no important uses

GLOSSARY

alloy
A mixture or combination of a metal and another substance (or more than one). Brass is an alloy of copper and zinc. Steels are alloys of iron and carbon, usually with other metals, like chromium or stainless steels.

carbon
A black substance that makes up soot and is used in alloys.

conductor
A substance that carries electricity (electrical conductor) or heat (thermal conductor) very well. Most metals do both.

corrosion
Becoming weakened, cracked and pitted with holes, especially when attacked by chemicals.

extraction
Getting a metal out of its ore (rock) by various processes, such as heating (smelting), pressure and treating with chemicals.

minerals
Naturally occurring substances that are of non-biological origin. They are usually crystalline. Rocks consist of many minerals.

ore
A rock or similar substance in the ground, which is worth digging up to obtain the metal from it.

radioactivity
Invisible rays and particles given off (radiated) by certain substances. These may cause harm to living things, such as sickness, and disease like cancers.

refining
Making a metal more pure, by removing other substances from it.

slag
Waste material left over from the mining process.

solder
An alloy used in molten form to join two metals together.